THE GRAND OSTRICH BALL

illustrated by
Peter Lawson

For Louise – P.L.

story by
Elizabeth Laird

For Angus – E.L.

HEINEMANN · LONDON

William Heinemann Ltd., Michelin House, 81 Fulham Road, London SW3 6RB LONDON   MELBOURNE   AUCKLAND
First published 1989 Illustrations copyright © Peter Lawson 1989 Text copyright © Elizabeth Laird 1989 ISBN 434 94741 5
Produced by Mandarin Offset , Printed and bound in Hong Kong All Rights Reserved

Zippi and Zac were having breakfast.
Zippi pecked at a bowl of nuts.
Zac reached for the sunflower seeds.
The clock struck eight.
"Time for work," said Zippi.
"Mustn't be late at the office."

Samson was there already.

"A letter for you," he said. Zac took it.

"From Africa," he said.

"Yes?" said Zippi.

"From the Ostrich Chief," said Zac.

"Well?" said Zippi.

"'Help'," read Zac.

"Help what?" said Zippi.

"Just 'help'," said Zac. "That's all it says."

Zippi took the letter.

"Aha," he said. "There's something in the corner.

It's the sign of the webbed foot.

The Mad Ducks are at it again."

"I'll phone FIFI," said Zac.

He dialled the number.

"Free International Flights Inc please," he said.

Zippi checked the safari rations.

"Must get a new nut-case," he said.

Samson rolled up the parachutes.

"You're sure to need these," he said.

Soon a crowd of migrating geese arrived.
"I refuse to ride on a goose," said Zac.
"It looks like you'll have to," said Zippi.
"FIFI's goofed again."

From up in the sky,
they had a bird's eye view of Africa.
"There's the ostrich!" shouted Zac.
"By the great Zambesi!"

"Hold on tight!" said Zippi.
"We're coming in to land."

The big ostrich stepped forward
and greeted Zippi.
"Welcome to Africa," he said.
"Thanks, Chief," said Zippi.
"What's going on?"

"It's those Mad Ducks again," said the Chief.

"They're nicking our tail feathers."

"What for?" said Zippi.

"For feather boas," said the Chief,

"to wear at the Mad Ducks' Ball."

Zac was disgusted.

"Nicking your tail feathers?" he said.

"Disgraceful! We'll soon put a stop to that.
We'll soon scare off your feather-nickers."

"Eh?" said the Chief. "Oh, yes, thanks."
"And now to business," said Zippi.
"Lead us to the scene of the crime."

The Chief took Zippi and Zac into a clearing.
"Look," said the Chief. "Over there."
The Mad Ducks were getting ready for the Ball.

Some were catching frogs for the feast.
Some were practising the can-can.

Some were dyeing ostrich feathers
and stitching them into boas.

"Aah!" said the Chief. "I can't bear to look!"
And he buried his head in the sand.

"There's only one thing to do," said Zippi.

"We must frighten them off."

Zac looked fierce and flapped his wings.

"Like this?" he said

"No," said Zippi, unzipping his safari kit.

"With this," and he
pulled out a lion's costume.

"You want me to dress up as a lion?" said Zac.
"Yes," said Zippi.
"You're mad," said Zac.
"No, the ducks are mad," said Zippi.
"I'm just crazy. Now get this costume on."

Zac was soon ready.

"OK, now roar," said Zippi.

"Erk," said Zac.

"Louder," said Zippi.

"Erk, erk," said Zac.

"Well, just do the best you can," said Zippi.

"ERK!" yelled Zac, and he made a wild dash
at the ducks.

The Mad Ducks shrieked with laughter.
"A toucan!" screamed one.
"Dressed as a lion!" roared another.
"Whatever next!" yelled a third.
"It's fancy dress," laughed a fourth.
"Good idea," said a fifth.

"I want to go in fancy dress," said one.

"I'll dress up as an ostrich," said another.

"Me too! Me too!" they all yelled.

"We need more feathers! We must go and find
the ostriches again."

Zac hopped back to Zippi.
"Did you hear that?" he said.
"They're going to steal more feathers!"
"Quick!" said Zippi. "We must try Plan Two."

And he pulled a snake
costume out of his safari kit.

"You want me to dress up as a snake?" said Zac.
"Yes," said Zippi.
"You're nuts," said Zac.
"No, but I like them," said Zippi.

Zac climbed into the costume.
It was a tight fit.

"Now hiss," said Zippi.

"Pff," said Zac.

"Louder," said Zippi.

"Pff, pff," said Zac.

"It will have to do," said Zippi.

"PFF!" yelled Zac.

and he made a wild dash at the ducks.

The Mad Ducks screamed with laughter.
"Oh look," said one,
"a toucan dressed up as a s . . . ."
"SNAKE!" another yelled in terror.

"Let's get out of here!" they shrieked together,
and suddenly the clearing was empty.
The Mad Ducks had flown away,
leaving hundreds of ostrich feathers behind them.

Zac was very pleased with himself.

"Was I good?" he said.

"You were terrific," said the Chief.

"Not bad," said Zippi, "but the real snake was better."

"What real snake?" said Zac.

"Never mind," said the Chief, quickly.
"I'd like to invite you both to the Ball."
"What Ball?" said Zac.
"The Ostrich Ball," said the Chief.
"The Mad Ducks left everything ready,
so let the party begin!"

Soon the Ball was in full swing.
Pretty young ostriches giggled and wriggled,
and waggled their tail-feathers.
"Look," said one of them to Zippi.

"I can can-can."
"Yahoo!" roared Zippi.
"A toucan can can-can too,"
and he danced off to join the fun.

"Oh my, what a party," said Zac, a few days later,
when they were safely back on the perch.

"It's all right for some," said Samson.

"I nearly forgot," said Zippi.

"I've got a present for you."

"Well, well," said Samson.

"Whoever saw a snail in a feather boa?"